MOSES

By Maud and Miska Petersham

An American ABC
America's Stamps
A Bird in the Hand
The Box with Red Wheels
The Boy Who Had No Heart
The Circus Baby
David
Jesus' Story
Joseph
Moses
My Very First Book
Off to Bed
The Rooster Crows
Ruth
The Silver Mace
The Story of Jesus
Story of the Presidents

MOSES

FROM THE STORY TOLD IN THE OLD TESTAMENT

MAUD and MISKA PETERSHAM

THE MACMILLAN COMPANY • NEW YORK • 1958

CONTENTS

While the Children of Israel were living in the land of Egypt, there came a new king over Egypt. He had never known Joseph and feared that the Israelites might become greater in number and more powerful than the Egyptians. So he set hard taskmasters over the Hebrews and made their lives bitter. Still they grew and multiplied.

THE HEBREW BABY

PHARAOH, the king of Egypt, feared that the children of Israel might become too great in the land. So he commanded that each boy baby born to the Hebrews must be killed.

A son was born to a certain woman of the Hebrews, and she hid him from the Egyptians

for three months. When she could no longer
hide him, she took an ark of bulrushes and
covered it with mud and pitch. She put her
child in the ark and left it among the reeds

that grew on the river's edge. A little girl, a sister of the baby, stood and watched to see what would happen to him.

The daughter of Pharaoh, the king, came down to bathe at the river and she and her maidens walked along by the river's edge. When she saw the ark among the reeds, she sent her maid to fetch it. And when she had opened it, she saw the child and the child was crying. She pitied the child and said, "This is one of the Hebrews' children."

Then the sister said to Pharaoh's daughter, "Shall I go and call a nurse of the Hebrew women, that she may nurse the child for thee?"

And Pharaoh's daughter said, "Go." And the sister went and called the child's mother.

And Pharaoh's daughter said to her, "Take this child away and nurse it for me, and I will give thee thy wages."

Then the mother took the child and cared for him. The child grew and she brought him to Pharaoh's daughter and he became like her own son. The daughter of Pharaoh called him Moses, and he grew up in her house.

THE BURNING BUSH

WHEN Moses was grown, he often went among his own people, the Hebrews. One day he saw an Egyptian striking one of his people, and he killed the Egyptian and hid his body in the sand.

Now when Pharaoh heard this, he wanted to kill Moses. But Moses fled to the land of Midian.

One day as he sat down by a well, seven sisters came to the well to draw water for their father's flocks. And shepherds came and drove them away, but Moses helped the sisters water their flocks.

When the girls told their father how Moses had helped them, the father sent for him. And Moses was content to dwell with this man. And he married one of the seven sisters.

While Moses was tending the flocks of his father-in-law in Midian, his own people in Egypt were slaves under hard taskmasters. They were forced to make bricks and build

great cities for the new Pharaoh. And they
cried to God, and God heard their cry.

One day as Moses led the flock, he came to a
mountain called The Mountain of God. Sud-
denly he saw a bush flaming with fire, but as
he watched, the bush was not burned. A voice
from the bush called, "Moses, Moses."

And Moses said, "Here am I."

The voice told him to put off his shoes from
his feet, for the place was holy ground. And
the voice said, "I am the God of thy father,

the God of Abraham, the God of Isaac, and the God of Jacob." And Moses hid his face, for he was afraid to look upon God.

And God said, "I have heard the cry of my people which are in Egypt, for I know their sorrows. And I am come down to deliver them, and to bring them up out of that land to a good land and a large land flowing with milk and honey."

Then God told Moses that he was the one chosen to go to Pharaoh and bring the Children of Israel out of Egypt. At first Moses was afraid that he would not be able to do this.

God promised to be with Moses and help him. He gave him a rod and showed him how with this rod he would be able to perform wonders. These wonders would prove to his people, and to the Egyptians, that it was God who had sent him.

God told Moses that his brother, Aaron, would be with him. Moses took the rod of God in his hand, and with his wife and his sons returned to Egypt. And Aaron came out to meet them.

THE TEN SIGNS

MOSES and Aaron went to Pharaoh and said, "Thus saith the Lord God of Israel, 'Let my people go, that they may hold a feast unto me in the wilderness.' "

And Pharaoh said, "Who is the Lord, that I should obey his voice to let Israel go? I know not the Lord, neither will I let Israel go."

That same day Pharaoh commanded that no more straw be given to the Hebrews with which to make the bricks. They must gather the straw themselves wherever they could find it, yet they must make just as many bricks as they did before.

So the Children of Israel were scattered through all the land searching for straw. When they could not make as many bricks as before, they were beaten by the taskmasters, and things seemed worse than before.

But God told Moses to go to Pharaoh and perform the signs. Then Pharaoh would know how great was the God of Israel and would let the Children of Israel go from Egypt.

So Moses and Aaron went to Pharaoh, and
when Pharaoh again refused to let them go,
Aaron cast down the rod of God before the
throne. And the rod became a serpent. But
Pharaoh would not listen.

Through Moses and Aaron, God gave other signs. The waters of Egypt were turned into blood. Still Pharaoh did not listen.

Frogs came up out of the waters and covered the land. And Pharaoh called upon Moses and Aaron to beg their God to destroy the frogs. He promised that he would then let the Children of Israel go. The frogs died out of the houses and out of the villages and out of the fields. But Pharaoh did not let the people go.

The dust was turned into lice, and swarms of flies covered the ground and filled the houses of the Egyptians. But still Pharaoh did not listen.

Moses and Aaron gave other signs. All the cattle of the Egyptians died, but not one of the cattle of the Children of Israel died. Boils broke out upon the men and the beasts of Egypt. Hail fell, locusts and thick darkness came, but only upon the Egyptians. Even then Pharaoh would not let the Children go from Egypt.

And then God said he would send one more sign. And it came to pass at midnight that all the first-born in the land of Egypt died, from the first-born of Pharaoh that sat upon his throne to the first-born of the captive that was in the dungeon, and all the first-born of the cattle. And Pharaoh rose up in the night, he and all his servants, and all the Egyptians. And there was a great cry in Egypt, for there was not a house where there was not one dead.

Then Pharaoh called for Moses and Aaron in the night and begged them to take the Children of Israel out of Egypt.

In great haste Moses and Aaron and all the Children of Israel and their flocks and their herds fled out of Egypt.

About six hundred thousand people, be-sides children, journeyed out on foot.

And God went before them to show them the way. He went in a pillar of cloud by day and a pillar of fire by night.

CROSSING THE RED SEA

IT was told to Pharaoh, the king, that the Israelites had fled. And then the Egyptians said to one another, "Why have we let the Israelites go from serving us?"

Pharaoh made ready his chariots and fol-lowed after them to bring them back. And he overtook them in their camp beside the sea.

When the Children of Israel saw the Egyp-tians coming after them, they were afraid and cried out to God. And Moses said, "Fear not, the Lord shall fight for you."

And Moses stretched out his hand over the sea, and God caused the sea to go back by a strong east wind all that night. And he made the sea dry land, and the waters were separated. And the Children of Israel went across the

sea upon dry ground. And there was a wall
of water upon their right hand and upon their
left.

And the Egyptians followed and went across
after them, even all Pharaoh's horses, his chariots, and his horsemen.

Then God told Moses to stretch out his hand again.

The waters returned to their place and covered the chariots and the horsemen and all the army of Pharaoh. There remained not so much as one of them.

THE WILDERNESS

AS the Children of Israel journeyed on from the Red Sea, they came into a wilderness. They found the water so bitter that they could not drink it. There was little food for so many people, and they complained against Moses and Aaron and wished that they were back in Egypt.

When Moses cried to God, God sweetened the water and sent them food. Each morning when the dew was gone, there lay on the ground small round things as small as the hoarfrost. Everyone gathered these and ate them and the taste was that of wafers made with honey. They called this food manna, and this was their bread in the wilderness.

As they went on, they again came to a place where there was no water. And the people complained against Moses and said, "Why hast thou brought us up out of Egypt to kill us and our children and our cattle with thirst?"

And Moses cried to God, saying, "What shall I do unto this people? They be almost ready to stone me."

And God told Moses to strike the rock with his rod. When Moses did this, a stream of water gushed from the rock, and the Children of Israel drank. And they made their camp around this rock.

While they were there, they were attacked by the people of Amalek who lived in that wilderness. Moses told one of the young men, Joshua, to choose men to go and fight Amalek.

During the battle, Moses took the rod of God in his hand and went to the top of a hill. And Aaron and Hur went with him. Now when Moses held up his hand with the rod, Israel won, and when he let down his hand, Amalek won.

But Moses was old and his hands grew tired.
So they took a stone and put it under him and
he sat on it. Then Aaron and Hur held up
his hands, one on the one side and one on the
other side. And his hands were steady until
the going down of the sun. And the Children
of Israel defeated Amalek.

THE COMMANDMENTS

IN the third month after the Children of Israel had gone out of the land of Egypt, they pitched their camp in the plain before Mount Sinai, the mountain of God.

God called Moses to the top of the mountain and Moses went up. There was a great cloud on the top of the mount, and the glory of God was over all, like fire. Here Moses stayed for forty days and forty nights.

And God spoke to Moses and gave him commandments and laws for the Children of Israel. And he gave him two tables of stone upon which the commandments were written.

When Moses delayed to come down out of the mount, the people did not know what had become of him. And they came to Aaron and asked him to make new gods for them to worship. They brought their golden earrings to Aaron. He melted them and shaped the melted gold into the form of a calf. He built an altar before it. And the people offered burnt offerings and feasted and danced.

God saw what was happening. He was angry and ready to destroy the Children of Israel. But Moses pleaded with God for Israel.

Moses came down from the mount with the two tables of stone in his hand. As he came near the camp, he saw the golden calf and the dancing. He was so angry that he cast the tables out of his hand and broke them on the rocks. He took the calf which they had made and burned it in the fire. He ground it into powder and threw it upon the water and made the Children of Israel drink of this water.

Moses stood at the entrance of the camp and called to him those who were on God's side. Then many of those who would not come were slain.

The next day Moses returned to God on the mount. He pleaded again for Israel, and God heard him.

Moses cut two tables out of stone like the first ones and carried them up into the mount. Again God wrote the commandments upon them. This time when Moses came down, his face shone with such a bright light that the

Children of Israel were afraid to come near him.

And Moses taught the Children of Israel the laws that God had given him.

THE WANDERINGS

THE Children of Israel journeyed on. At last they came near the land which God had promised them. And Moses sent men to spy out this land. After forty days these men

returned and reported that it was a very good land. They brought back a cluster of grapes so large that two men had to carry it upon a staff. But they said that the people who already lived in the land were strong and had many walled cities.

Then the Children of Israel were afraid to go over into this land. They forgot that God was with them. They cried out and wanted to return to Egypt.

Then God said, "How long will this people provoke me, and how long will it be before they believe in me?" And he would have destroyed them but for the pleading of Moses.

Then God told them, because they still did not believe after all he had done, they should never see the land which he had promised to them. They should die in the wilderness and only their children should ever reach the land of Canaan.

God caused them to turn back into the desert. And from that time the Children of Israel wandered in the wilderness for nearly forty years.

In their wanderings they came again to a place where there was no water, and God told Moses to take the rod in his hand and speak to the rock.

Moses was angry with the people and he struck the rock twice. "Hear me, ye rebels," he cried. "Must we fetch you water out of this rock?" And he gave no glory to God.

God was displeased with this and told Moses that he should only lead the people to the border of the Promised Land, but that he would not be allowed to go over into it.

THE DEATH OF MOSES

AFTER the forty years of wandering were over, the Children of Israel again came to the border of the Promised Land. Moses called the leaders of the twelve tribes together and talked with them and blessed them. He laid his hand upon Joshua and gave his leadership over to him.

Then Moses went up alone from the plains of Moab to the top of the mountain of Nebo.

And God showed him all the land of Canaan as it stretched to the sea. And he showed him the plain of the valley of Jericho, the city of palm trees.

And God said, "This is the land which I promised. I have caused you to see it with your eyes, but you shall not go over into it."

So Moses, the servant of the Lord, died there on the mountain top. There was never after a prophet in the land of Israel like Moses, whom God knew face to face.

After the death of Moses, Joshua led the Children of Israel into the land of Canaan, the Promised Land.